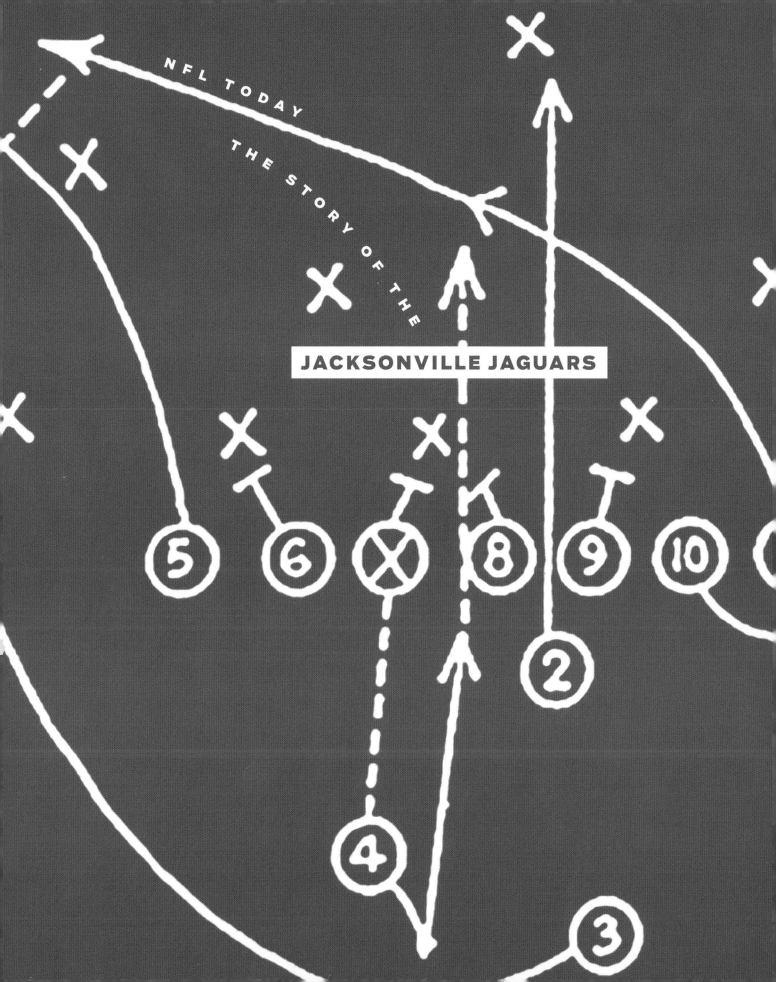

NFL TODAY

THE STORY OF THE JACKSONVILLE JAGUARS

NATE FRISCH

CREATIVE EDUCATION

PUBLISHED BY CREATIVE EDUCATION
P.O. BOX 227, MANKATO, MINNESOTA 56002
CREATIVE EDUCATION IS AN IMPRINT OF THE CREATIVE COMPANY
WWW.THECREATIVECOMPANY.US

DESIGN AND PRODUCTION BY BLUE DESIGN
ART DIRECTION BY RITA MARSHALL
PRINTED IN THE UNITED STATES OF AMERICA

PHOTOGRAPHS BY CORBIS (CHARLES W. LAZIER/
REUTERS, JOHN RAOUX/AP), GETTY IMAGES
(DOUG BENC, JOHN BIEVER/SPORTS ILLUSTRATED,
NEIL BRAKE/AFP, PAUL K. BUCK/AFP, DAVID
DRAPKIN, STEPHEN DUNN, BILL FRAKES/SPORTS
ILLUSTRATED, LARRY FRENCH, CHRIS GRAYTHEN,
SAM GREENWOOD, OTTO GREULE JR./ALLSPORT,
MICHAEL HICKEY, SIMEONE HUBER, ANDY LYONS,
ANDY LYONS/ALLSPORT, DAVID MAXWELL/AFP, AL
MESSERSCHMIDT, JOE ROBBINS, ELIOT J. SCHECHTER,
JAMIE SQUIRE, ROBERT SULLIVAN/AFP, JOE TRAVER/
TIME & LIFE PICTURES, CHRIS TROTMAN)

LIBRARY OF CONGRESS CATALOGING-IN-PUBLICATION DATA
FRISCH, NATE.
THE STORY OF THE JACKSONVILLE JAGUARS / BY NATE FRISCH.
P. CM. — (NFL TODAY)
INCLUDES INDEX.
SUMMARY: THE HISTORY OF THE NATIONAL FOOTBALL LEAGUE'S
JACKSONVILLE JAGUARS, SURVEYING THE FRANCHISE'S BIGGEST
STARS AND MOST MEMORABLE MOMENTS FROM ITS INAUGURAL
SEASON IN 1995 TO TODAY.
ISBN 978-1-60818-306-7
1. JACKSONVILLE JAGUARS (FOOTBALL TEAM)—HISTORY—
JUVENILE LITERATURE. I. TITLE.

GV956.J33F75 2013
796.332'640975912—DC23   2012031215

FIRST EDITION
9 8 7 6 5 4 3 2 1

COVER: WIDE RECEIVER JUSTIN BLACKMON
PAGE 2: RUNNING BACK MAURICE JONES-DREW
PAGES 4–5: 2008 JACKSONVILLE JAGUARS DEFENSE
PAGE 6: DEFENSIVE BACK BRIAN WITHERSPOON

TABLE OF CONTENTS

JACKSONVILLE HAS A HISTORY AS AN IMPORTANT SHIPPING PORT

Florida Dreaming

Jacksonville, Florida, lies in the northeast corner of the state along the Atlantic Ocean and near the Georgia border. Named after General Andrew Jackson, who was Florida's first military governor (and later became United States president), Jacksonville's first purpose was that of a distribution center for transporting the Southeast's citrus and sugar crops. As time went on, the region's mild winter climate made it appealing as a tourist destination and movie-making location. Today, Jacksonville also has the unique distinction of covering more land (874 square miles) than any other city in the continental U.S.

Despite its sprawling size and the fact that it is Florida's most populous city, Jacksonville was without any major professional sports franchises late into the 20th century. That changed when the Jaguars of the National Football League (NFL) were created to represent the Florida city. And although the team first hit the field in 1995, the process of obtaining a franchise required years of hard work from the club's owners.

POWERFUL OFFENSIVE TACKLE TONY BOSELLI HELPED FORM JACKSONVILLE'S FOUNDATION

Kevin Hardy

LINEBACKER / JAGUARS SEASONS: 1996–2001 / HEIGHT: 6-FOOT-4 / WEIGHT: 259 POUNDS

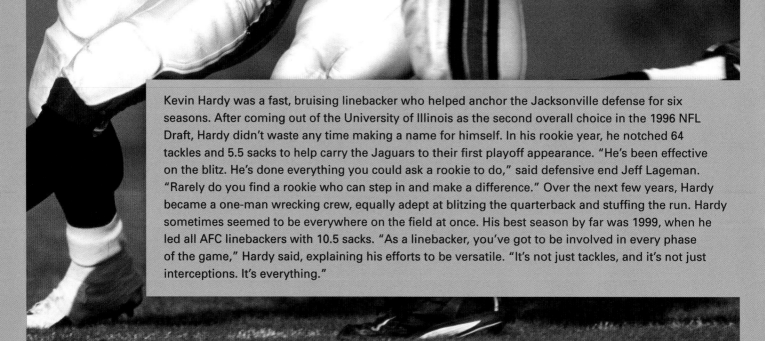

Kevin Hardy was a fast, bruising linebacker who helped anchor the Jacksonville defense for six seasons. After coming out of the University of Illinois as the second overall choice in the 1996 NFL Draft, Hardy didn't waste any time making a name for himself. In his rookie year, he notched 64 tackles and 5.5 sacks to help carry the Jaguars to their first playoff appearance. "He's been effective on the blitz. He's done everything you could ask a rookie to do," said defensive end Jeff Lageman. "Rarely do you find a rookie who can step in and make a difference." Over the next few years, Hardy became a one-man wrecking crew, equally adept at blitzing the quarterback and stuffing the run. Hardy sometimes seemed to be everywhere on the field at once. His best season by far was 1999, when he led all AFC linebackers with 10.5 sacks. "As a linebacker, you've got to be involved in every phase of the game," Hardy said, explaining his efforts to be versatile. "It's not just tackles, and it's not just interceptions. It's everything."

JIMMY SMITH POSTED 7 STRAIGHT SEASONS OF AT LEAST 1,000 RECEIVING YARDS

In the late 1980s, the NFL announced it would be awarding expansion franchises to two cities that could present the most compelling cases for hosting a team. In August 1989, a group called "Touchdown Jacksonville!"—led by millionaire businessmen Thomas Petway and J. Wayne Weaver—was formed with the goal of proving that Jacksonville had the resources and fan base to support a team. The prospective owners went so far as to hold a team-naming contest before they even knew they'd have a club to bear the title. Jaguars was the most popular suggestion, named after the stealthy and muscular big cats. The years of work paid off, and in 1993, the NFL announced that Jacksonville and Charlotte, North Carolina, would receive the new expansion franchises.

Jacksonville hired Tom Coughlin as the Jaguars' first head coach. As an assistant coach for the Green Bay Packers and New York Giants, Coughlin had developed a reputation as a demanding, no-nonsense leader. The Jacksonville front office thought he was perfect for molding a new team, and Coughlin was given control over all draft choices and player signings. "I wouldn't have done it any other way," Coughlin said. "These days, it's imperative to have control of your team's direction and personnel."

In February 1995, the NFL held an expansion draft in which the Jaguars and the Carolina Panthers were allowed to select some players from the existing 28 NFL franchises. Jacksonville chose veteran quarterback Steve Beuerlein and defensive lineman Paul Frase as well as explosive wide receiver Jimmy Smith. After the expansion draft, Coughlin put together the franchise's first trade. He sent two draft picks to Green Bay for Mark Brunell, a young, left-handed quarterback known for his quick feet.

oach Coughlin felt that the "heart and soul" of a football team was the offensive line. So, with the team's first pick in the 1995 NFL Draft, Jacksonville selected offensive tackle Tony Boselli, a former All-American at the University of Southern California. In addition to Boselli, the Jaguars used a first-round pick to select running back James Stewart out of the University of Tennessee.

On September 3, 1995, more than 72,000 fans packed into Jacksonville Municipal Stadium to watch the new team in teal and gold take the field for the first time. The Jaguars lost the game to the Houston Oilers, 10–3, but Jacksonville fans cheered wildly just the same.

In the fifth game of the season, Jacksonville faced the Oilers in Houston's Astrodome, and Brunell stepped in for the struggling Beuerlein in the fourth quarter with Jacksonville down 16–10. Brunell rallied the team, leading the offense down the field and ending the drive with a 15-yard strike to wide receiver Desmond Howard for the win. One week after that, the Jaguars won their first home game. The 20–16 upset over the Pittsburgh Steelers would seem even more special after the season when the Steelers marched all the way to the Super Bowl.

Although Jacksonville finished its inaugural season just 4–12, it fought hard every week, losing five games by seven points or fewer. Boselli and tackle Brian DeMarco anchored a stout offensive line, and

Touchdown Jacksonville!

In 1989, Touchdown Jacksonville! was formed to lure an NFL franchise to Jacksonville. A year later, NFL commissioner Paul Tagliabue announced that the league would expand by two teams for the 1995 season. The group quickly got to work, but the northeastern Florida city was considered a long shot because of its relatively small media market and the fact that two NFL teams, the Tampa Bay Buccaneers and Miami Dolphins, and three major college teams already called Florida home. But that wasn't the only trouble. Touchdown Jacksonville! had financial problems, leading many members of the group to drop out. At one point in 1993, after the Jacksonville city council denied funds for a stadium, the group closed its offices. A month later, however, encouraged by NFL officials, Touchdown Jacksonville! got back in the race. On November 30 of that year, Jacksonville was awarded the NFL's 30th franchise. The next day, a helicopter landed at midfield of Gator Bowl Stadium, which was initially intended to be the home of the new team, and majority owner Wayne Weaver stepped onto the field to celebrate with 25,000 cheering fans.

WAYNE WEAVER OWNED THE JAGUARS FRANCHISE FROM 1993 TO 2011

KEENAN McCARDELL PLAYED FOR FIVE NFL TEAMS BUT WAS BEST IN JACKSONVILLE

Brunell proved to be one of the American Football Conference's (AFC) most exciting quarterbacks. "I studied players throughout the 1994 season, and I was excited about Mark's athleticism, his toughness, his ability to move in the pocket, and his arm strength," Coughlin said of his quarterback. "I just felt like this would be the guy that we would want to lead our team."

In the months before their second season, the Jaguars continued to add talent. Among the key offensive additions were wide receiver Keenan McCardell. Defensively, the team added bite by bringing in hard-hitting linebacker Kevin Hardy. As the 1996 season drew near, the Jaguars and their fans were dreaming big.

Jimmy Smith

WIDE RECEIVER / JAGUARS SEASONS: 1995–2005 / HEIGHT: 6-FOOT-1 / WEIGHT: 208 POUNDS

Before arriving in Jacksonville, Jimmy Smith experienced a bumpy road in his first years as an NFL wide receiver. Coming out of Mississippi's Jackson State University, he spent two years with the Dallas Cowboys and Philadelphia Eagles before being picked up by the expansion Jaguars. By 1996, he was the most dominant receiver on the team, blowing past defenders, making spectacular grabs, and helping power the Jaguars all the way to the AFC Championship Game. One of his greatest highlights occurred in a 1998 playoff game against the New England Patriots. In the fourth quarter, with Jacksonville leading 12–10, Smith broke away from defensive back Ty Law and made a diving catch in the back of the end zone that helped Jacksonville secure the win. In 2005, after 13 NFL seasons, the five-time Pro-Bowler ended his career with 12,287 receiving yards. "We nicknamed him 'J-Smooth' because he made everything look so easy," said Baltimore Ravens cornerback Chris McAlister. "Jimmy was clearly one of the best receivers on the field. He was one of the most consistent players in the NFL, with his great combination of speed and power."

Brunell's Big Scramble

On January 4, 1997, in the second round of the AFC playoffs, the Jaguars faced the mighty 13–3 Denver Broncos at Mile High Stadium, a place where Denver had not lost a playoff game in 13 years. Few people gave the second-year Jags much of a chance to win. But by halftime, Jacksonville held a slim 13–12 lead. In the third quarter, Jacksonville quarterback Mark Brunell threw a 31-yard touchdown pass to receiver Keenan McCardell, and in the fourth quarter, the Jaguars led 23–12. But quarterback John Elway and the Broncos came back, scoring a touchdown and a two-point conversion to tighten the game to 23–20. With the lead in jeopardy and Jacksonville at midfield, Brunell nearly got sacked, but he squirted away from the Denver defense. He raced right, dodged a safety, swerved left, got a block from McCardell, and scrambled all the way to Denver's 21-yard line. The highlight-reel play set up another touchdown that secured a 30–27 upset for Jacksonville. "He made huge plays all day," Elway said afterward. "You don't see a lot of guys who can make things happen like he can."

MARK BRUNELL WAS ONE OF THE BEST SCRAMBLING QUARTERBACKS OF HIS ERA.

A Mighty Roar

Jacksonville's second season started with a whimper, as the team reached the midway point with a mere 3–5 record. But on November 24, the Jaguars topped the Baltimore Ravens 28–25 in an overtime thriller. That game seemed to energize the young Jaguars, who reeled off five straight victories to end the season. Incredibly, in only its second season, the team had put together a 9–7 record and made the playoffs. "[People] around the nation didn't know who we are," said kicker Mike Hollis, whose 42-yard field goal in the last game of the season earned the team a postseason berth. "But they know now."

But the Jaguars weren't content to just make the playoffs. In the first round, on the road against the Buffalo Bills, big running back Natrone Means rumbled for 175 yards, and Hollis banked a late fourth-quarter, 45-yard field goal off the uprights

AT ALMOST 250 POUNDS, NATRONE MEANS WAS A SLEDGEHAMMER OF A BALLCARRIER

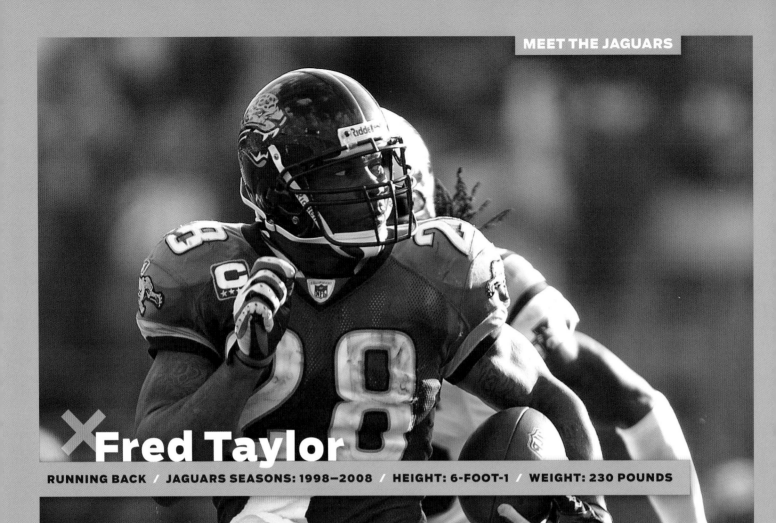

Fred Taylor

RUNNING BACK / JAGUARS SEASONS: 1998–2008 / HEIGHT: 6-FOOT-1 / WEIGHT: 230 POUNDS

For more than a decade, Fred Taylor was the face of the Jacksonville Jaguars as he slashed and sliced through opposing defenses. The physical but surprisingly shifty running back was acquired in the first round of the NFL Draft in 1998 and promptly ran for 1,223 yards as a rookie. In one game in December 2006 against the Indianapolis Colts, Taylor broke loose on the first play from scrimmage for a 76-yard run. Later, in the second quarter, he dashed around the end of the line and made a spin move between Colts defenders Matt Giordano and Martin Jackson, who ended up tackling each other instead of the elusive Taylor. "We're not sure where Fred is going to run, but we just [block] our guys and let him go where he wants with the ball," said Jaguars offensive tackle Zach Wiegert. "It's a great feeling blocking for a guy like that, because you know he's going to make you look good." Even though Taylor averaged more than 1,000 rushing yards a year in his first 10 seasons, he was not named to the Pro Bowl until 2007.

"You know he's going to make you look good."

ZACH WIEGERT ON BLOCKING
FOR FRED TAYLOR

to upset the Bills 30–27. The surprises kept coming the next week as the Jaguars stunned the Denver Broncos 30–27 in Denver's Mile High Stadium. In that game, Brunell shredded the Broncos' defense with 245 passing yards. Unbelievably, Jacksonville was just one win away from the Super Bowl.

Although they couldn't quite complete the dream season—losing the AFC Championship Game 20–6 to the New England Patriots—the Jaguars had opened eyes around the NFL. On the season, James Stewart had teamed up with Means to post a combined 1,230 rushing yards, while speedy receiver Jimmy Smith caught 83 passes for 1,244 yards. After the Jaguars' amazing run, Coughlin was named NFL Coach of the Year.

The Jaguars began the 1997 season determined to show the world that 1996 hadn't been a fluke. Although the team was dealt a serious blow when Brunell went down with a knee injury before the season, backup quarterbacks Steve Matthews and Rob Johnson stepped in to guide the team to a 2–0 start.

The Jags continued to roll after Brunell returned to the lineup. McCardell and Smith each posted more than 1,000 receiving yards on the season and, in the process, became popularly known as "Thunder and Lightning." McCardell was "Thunder" because of his willingness to run routes up the dangerous, linebacker-patrolled middle of the field and his clutch third-down catches. Smith was "Lightning" because of his greater speed. Stewart also starred, earning a special place in Jacksonville's record books by scoring five touchdowns in a 38–21 victory over the Philadelphia Eagles. Thanks to these efforts, Jacksonville finished the year 11–5 and returned to the playoffs.

In the postseason, Jacksonville faced Denver once again. The Broncos had revenge on their minds and got it, routing the Jaguars 42–17. Despite the loss, the young Jacksonville franchise was riding high,

A Blowout Season

The Jaguars enjoyed their greatest season ever in 1999, when the five-year-old franchise went 14–2. The record was not only the best in Jaguars history, but it was also the best in the NFL that year. Jacksonville dominated teams throughout the season, but the Jaguars' most spectacular win that year occurred in the playoffs, when they blew out the Miami Dolphins 62–7. Before the game, skeptics had questioned Jacksonville's legitimacy, noting that none of its 14 wins had come against teams with winning records. Quarterback Mark Brunell silenced those critics on the opening series by engineering a 73-yard touchdown drive. On Jacksonville's third possession, running back Fred Taylor busted through the right end, slipped through Miami's defenders, and sprinted 90 yards for a touchdown. By halftime, the score was 41–7, Jacksonville. All told, the Jaguars racked up 520 yards of offense, forced 7 Miami turnovers, and held the Dolphins to only 131 yards of offense. "It was a great day for the Jaguars," Jacksonville coach Tom Coughlin said. "I think we all understand a little bit better what home-field advantage is all about, because our stadium was rocking and rolling today."

A QUICK-MOVING, 225-POUND SAFETY, DONOVIN DARIUS HIT LIKE A TRUCK

having made the playoffs twice in three years. "It's no secret," Michael Huyghue, Jacksonville's vice president of football operations, said of the team's success. "We thought we would try to grow the team on a three-year basis, so that the young players we had could mature to the peaks of their careers in that third year."

The Jaguars began the 1998 season 5–0, but then injuries to Brunell and Stewart threatened to derail the season. Luckily, rookie running back Fred Taylor stepped in to ignite the offense. On his very first carry as a starter, Taylor raced 52 yards for a touchdown. In another game against the Tampa Bay Buccaneers, with the Jaguars trailing 24–23 and less than three minutes to play, Taylor ran up the middle, cut back to the right, then outran Tampa Bay defenders for 70 yards to score the game-winning touchdown. "Fred gives us an added dimension we've never had before," said tight end Rich Griffith. "When he gets going, we're hard to stop." It would be a banner year for the young runner as he ended the season with 1,223 rushing yards and 17 touchdowns.

Jacksonville's defense, meanwhile, remained one of the NFL's fiercest, thanks to end Joel Smeenge, linebacker Bryce Paup, and hard-hitting rookie safety Donovin Darius. By the end of the season, Jacksonville was 11–5 and back in the postseason. In the first round of the playoffs, Taylor tore through

FRED TAYLOR GALLOPED TO 37 TOUCHDOWNS IN ALL FROM 1998 TO 2000

the Patriots' defense for 162 yards as the Jags won 25–10. A week later, however, the team fell to the New York Jets, 34–24.

Jacksonville came back hungrier than ever in 1999. The Jaguars' defense was the NFL's stingiest, giving up just 13.6 points per game. Defensive end Tony Brackens and cornerback Aaron Beasley were particularly disruptive, tallying 12 sacks and 6 interceptions respectively. Meanwhile, the offense held its own. Stewart and Taylor pounded the ball for 19 touchdowns, and Smith recorded a career-high 116 receptions for 1,636 yards. Jacksonville's full-team effort led to a stunning 14–2 record.

After a first-round playoff bye, the Jaguars looked unstoppable in round two, crushing the Miami Dolphins 62–7. For the second time in their short history, the Jaguars were just one win away from the Super Bowl. Only the Tennessee Titans—the team that had handed the Jaguars both of their regular-season losses—stood in their way. The Titans again had their number, beating the Jags 33–14.

Home of the Jags

In November 1993, when the NFL officially awarded Jacksonville a new franchise, the city's first order of business was to find a home for the new team. Since Gator Bowl Stadium was already 45 years old, the city decided to demolish it and built a new arena. The Jaguars and the city of Jacksonville spent $134 million, and in slightly more than 19 months, Jacksonville Municipal Stadium was completed in time for opening day in 1995. It was the first time in NFL history that an expansion team played its first season in a brand-new stadium. The stadium, which could hold more than 67,000 fans, featured two 156-foot-wide scoreboards anchored at each end zone. In 1997, Alltel Communications bought a 10-year naming contract, and the field became Alltel Stadium. In 2005, it hosted Super Bowl XXXIX. For the event, the city spent an additional $63 million on improvements, including the addition of escalators in the stands above each end zone. In 2007, after Alltel's contract ended, the stadium went back to being called Jacksonville Municipal Stadium until 2010, when it took on the name EverBank Field.

SINCE JACKSONVILLE'S STADIUM OPENED, ALMOST 4,000 SEATS HAVE BEEN ADDED

STACEY MACK EXCELLED AT BLASTING INTO THE END ZONE FROM CLOSE RANGE

Thunder, Lightning, and Drama

In 2000, the Jaguars continued to roll. In the first game of the season, they defeated the Cleveland Browns 27–7 on the road behind their Thunder and Lightning duo, which combined for almost 170 receiving yards. Although Smith and McCardell would shine all season long (each would post more than 1,200 receiving yards), and Taylor would set a team rushing record with 1,399 yards, the Jaguars slipped to 7–9, their first losing season in five years.

The 2001 season again started well, as the Jaguars went 2–0. While an injured Taylor missed most of the season, backup running back Stacey Mack and veteran tight end Kyle Brady helped pick up the slack. Smith also continued to cement his status as one of the league's best wide receivers. In one midseason game, he caught 15 passes for 291 yards against the Ravens, and he finished the year with more than 100 receptions. Still, the Jags went just 6–10.

AT 280 POUNDS, KYLE BRADY WAS TOUGH TO STOP WITH THE BALL IN HIS HANDS

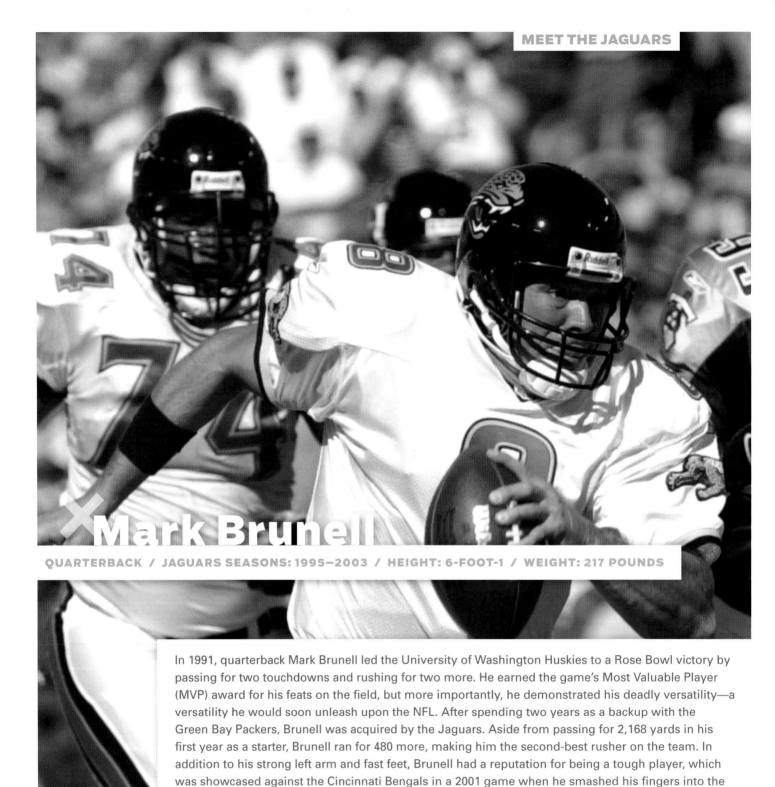

Mark Brunell

QUARTERBACK / JAGUARS SEASONS: 1995–2003 / HEIGHT: 6-FOOT-1 / WEIGHT: 217 POUNDS

In 1991, quarterback Mark Brunell led the University of Washington Huskies to a Rose Bowl victory by passing for two touchdowns and rushing for two more. He earned the game's Most Valuable Player (MVP) award for his feats on the field, but more importantly, he demonstrated his deadly versatility—a versatility he would soon unleash upon the NFL. After spending two years as a backup with the Green Bay Packers, Brunell was acquired by the Jaguars. Aside from passing for 2,168 yards in his first year as a starter, Brunell ran for 480 more, making him the second-best rusher on the team. In addition to his strong left arm and fast feet, Brunell had a reputation for being a tough player, which was showcased against the Cincinnati Bengals in a 2001 game when he smashed his fingers into the facemask of a defender. With his fingers cut and bleeding, Brunell went straight back onto the field and threw a perfect, 27-yard strike to set up the game-winning touchdown. "I didn't think he was going to go back," said receiver Jimmy Smith. "When he did, it inspired the guys. Mark makes this team go."

"Mark makes this team go."

JIMMY SMITH ON MARK BRUNELL

Facing salary cap limitations, the Jaguars said goodbye to Tony Boselli and Seth Payne in the off-season. They also let McCardell go, breaking up the NFL's most lethal receiving tandem. When the 2002 Jaguars posted another 6–10 record, team ownership decided that a change was needed at the top as well, and Coughlin was replaced as head coach by former NFL linebacker Jack Del Rio. Despite being only 39 years old, Del Rio had been defensive coordinator for the Carolina Panthers, where he had taken a last-place defense and turned it into one of the league's best in just one year. "We're going to put the intensity back in this stadium," Del Rio promised the Jacksonville faithful.

Before the 2003 season, the Jaguars drafted Byron Leftwich, a big (6-foot-5 and 245 pounds) and confident quarterback who had been a star at Marshall University. Brunell was beginning to slow down, and the team hoped that Leftwich—along with other talented additions such as veteran defensive end Hugh Douglas and linebacker Mike Peterson—would lead the Jaguars back among the AFC's elite.

The 2003 season started badly for the Jaguars, with four straight losses. Even worse, Brunell was sidelined by an elbow injury in the third game, forcing Leftwich into the starting lineup earlier than planned. Although shaky at first, he showed poise in the fifth game of the season against the San Diego Chargers. In the fourth quarter, with less than 3 minutes to play and the ball at the Jaguars' 10-yard line, Leftwich rolled out and threw a pass to Taylor, who broke loose and dashed 60 yards for a touchdown, securing a 27–21 victory. Even though Brunell eventually healed, Coach Del Rio decided to stay with the rookie. Leftwich made plenty of mistakes, and the Jaguars finished a mere 5–11, but Jags fans had reason to hope as their new quarterback gained valuable experience and the Jacksonville "D" finished as the NFL's second-best run defense, allowing an average of just 87 yards a game.

During the off-season, Jacksonville traded Brunell to the Washington Redskins. The team also continued to add young talent, signing star safety Deon Grant from the Carolina Panthers and selecting wide receiver Reggie Williams with the ninth overall pick in the 2004 NFL Draft.

Leftwich led the Jaguars to a fast 3–0 start in 2004, with all of the victories coming by three points or fewer. The most dramatic win came in the season's first game, at Buffalo. With time expiring, Leftwich threw a seven-yard pass to rookie wide receiver Ernest Wilford, who made a leaping catch between three Bills defenders to give the Jaguars the victory. "Good teams find a way to win, and we want to become a good team," said Del Rio.

The rest of the season was

BYRON LEFTWICH WAS A VERY SLOW RUNNER BUT SHOWED STRONG LEADERSHIP SKILLS

Tony Boselli

OFFENSIVE TACKLE / JAGUARS SEASONS: 1995–2001 / HEIGHT: 6-FOOT-7 / WEIGHT: 325 POUNDS

Tony Boselli was widely regarded as one of the NFL's finest offensive tackles of the 1990s. He was one of those rare offensive linemen both quick enough to excel at pass protection and strong enough to blast open holes for running backs. During his college career at the University of Southern California, Boselli was a first-team All-American in 1994 and 1995. He was the first player ever to be drafted by the Jaguars and went on to make the Pro Bowl five times. He played seven seasons for the Jaguars before being picked by the Houston Texans in the NFL's 2002 expansion draft, but injuries forced him to retire just a year later. On March 21, 2006, he signed a one-day contract with Jacksonville so he could officially retire as part of the team. Soon after, he became the first player to be inducted into the Jaguars' Ring of Honor. "It's appropriate to have Tony as the first member of the Ring of Honor as one of the all-time great Jaguars," said team owner Wayne Weaver. "Others will follow later, but Tony will be the first."

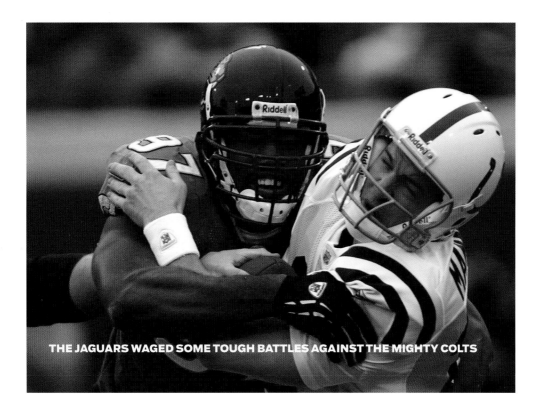

THE JAGUARS WAGED SOME TOUGH BATTLES AGAINST THE MIGHTY COLTS

a roller-coaster ride for Jacksonville. The Jaguars captured last-minute wins against the Indianapolis Colts and Kansas City Chiefs. But they also suffered painful losses such as a late-season, 21–0 defeat at home to the Houston Texans, which knocked them out of the playoffs. Still, the team improved to 9–7, putting Jacksonville back in the hunt.

With the same key position players in place, the Jaguars hoped the steadily improving Leftwich could lead the 2005 squad into the playoffs. It appeared as though that was exactly what would happen as the Jaguars roared to a strong start behind the confident leadership of the young quarterback. But in a Week 12 matchup against the Arizona Cardinals, Leftwich was sidelined with a broken ankle.

Unexpectedly, backup quarterback David Garrard stepped into the lineup and caught the Cardinals' defense off-guard by rushing for 61 yards and a touchdown in a 24–17 victory. He went on to orchestrate four more wins, and the Jaguars finished with an impressive 12–4 record. Leftwich had recovered from his injury before the team's playoff game against the Patriots, and Del Rio was faced with a tough decision: start the quarterback who led the team to a 7–3 start or the one who guided it to a 5–1 finish. Del Rio chose Leftwich, and Jacksonville was destroyed by New England, 28–3.

In the off-season, 37-year-old Jimmy Smith—one of the original Jaguars—retired despite still being the team's best receiver. "It's hard because I know I can still go out there and do it," Smith said. "I just figure it's not in my heart to [continue].... It's best for me to leave on a high note."

GEORGE WRIGHSTER (LEFT) AND MATT JONES WERE HUGE JAGUARS PASSING TARGETS

JACKSONVILLE CAPTURED ITS SIXTH OVERALL PLAYOFF BERTH IN 2007

The Jags Find Their MoJo

In 2006, Leftwich again began the season as the starter and again was replaced by Garrard after an ankle injury. Neither played as well as he had the previous season, but the offense got a boost from rookie running back Maurice Jones-Drew. "MoJo" was 5-foot-7, built like a bowling ball, and had surprising speed and power. In his first year, he rushed for 13 touchdowns, caught 46 passes, and returned a kickoff 93 yards for a score. Behind the one-two punch of the veteran Taylor and young Jones-Drew, the Jaguars scored about 100 points more than they gave up that year but somehow managed only an 8–8 record, losing their final 3 games by a touchdown or less.

Before the 2007 season, the Jaguars made a permanent switch to Garrard at quarterback, and he had the best year of his career, completing 64 percent of his passes for 18 touchdowns and only 3 interceptions. The Jags' running back duo continued to

DAVID GARRARD SPENT HIS ENTIRE PRO CAREER WEARING A JACKSONVILLE UNIFORM

A Performance Unappreciated

After the 2008 season, running back Fred Taylor—the longtime face of the Jaguars franchise—departed Jacksonville. This left Maurice Jones-Drew as the team's featured back. "MoJo" had already shown off his combination of agility, speed, and power while splitting time with Taylor, but some skeptics wondered if the 5-foot-7 halfback could endure a full-time load of carries. On November 1, 2009, against the division rival Tennessee Titans, Jones-Drew carried the ball only 8 times ... for 177 yards and 2 touchdowns. The explosive performance included an 80-yard scamper during which the shifty runner dodged 5 would-be tacklers and shrugged off another on his way to the end zone. He followed that up with a 79-yard touchdown dash that he began by muscling through 3 tackles near the line of scrimmage. Jones-Drew became just the third player in NFL history with 2 rushing touchdowns of 75 or more yards in a game, and the day may have gone down as one of the great moments in team history, if not for one problem: Titans running back Chris Johnson ran for 228 yards against the Jaguars' defense, and Jacksonville lost 30–13.

RUSHING OR BLOCKING, MAURICE JONES-DREW (LEFT) SHOWED GREAT POWER

impress, and Jacksonville went 11–5 and earned a spot in the postseason as an AFC Wild Card team.

Garrard struggled in an opening-round playoff matchup against the Pittsburgh Steelers, but Jones-Drew kept the offense afloat by scoring a rushing and receiving touchdown and returning a kickoff 96 yards. The defense—led by cornerback Rashean Mathis—also came up big, sacking Steelers quarterback Ben Roethlisberger six times and intercepting three of his passes. After giving up a 28–10 lead in the fourth quarter, Jacksonville scored a field goal in the final minute to hang on to a 31–29 victory. Next it faced the Patriots, who'd made the NFL history books by going undefeated in the regular season. New

BY 2013, RASHEAN MATHIS HAD NOTCHED 30 CAREER INTERCEPTIONS

GUARD VINCE MANUWAI PROVIDED EIGHT YEARS OF SOLID PASS PROTECTION

England continued its winning streak, felling the Jaguars 31–20.

After the season, the Jaguars rewarded Garrard's play with a contract extension. But in 2008, he was sacked twice as many times and threw four times as many interceptions. Many other Jaguars also seemed to play flat. "We have some outstanding players, but the mix is bad," Taylor said after the team's 4–7 start. "We can't really find that chemistry that we need." Things only got worse. Jacksonville finished 5–11, and longtime standout Fred Taylor left the team after the season.

The Jaguars showed some signs of improvement the next two seasons. Jones-Drew rushed for more than 1,300 yards in both 2009 and 2010. Big, speedy cornerback Derek Cox intercepted 8 passes and batted down 19 more in his first 2 seasons as a pro. And Garrard threw a career-high 23 touchdowns in 2010. But overall, the Jaguars lacked the talent of previous years and went a mediocre 15–17, missing the playoffs both years.

Del Rio and the Jaguars' front office hoped their postseason prospects would improve in 2011 when they selected quarterback Blaine Gabbert with the 10th overall pick in the NFL Draft. Gabbert was a big passer who had demonstrated good mobility and a strong arm while playing college ball at the University of Missouri. However, while his natural gifts were apparent, he struggled to consistently lead the Jacksonville offense, throwing just 12 touchdowns and 11 interceptions as a rookie. The 2011 Jaguars

Mustache Mania

Wayne Weaver was the primary owner of the Jacksonville Jaguars from the franchise's inception in 1993, but Weaver sold the club near the end of the 2011 season. The buyer was Illinois businessman Shahid Khan. Khan was born in Pakistan and, from humble beginnings, worked hard to make his fortune in America. Jacksonville fans appreciated his blue-collar beginnings, but what really stood out about the new owner was his mustache. "That mustache didn't come out of nowhere. That's his signature," said a longtime acquaintance of Khan about his meticulously groomed facial hair. Although Khan would not take over the franchise until 2012, fans eagerly embraced his waxed whiskers, and soon T-shirts were being sold that featured a mustachioed team logo. The biggest show of "'stache support" came during a nationally televised Monday night game in December. Leading up to the contest, Khanesque mustache cutouts were posted online by a local newspaper and handed out at the stadium. While Khan was not in attendance for the prime-time event, his trademark feature was well represented by thousands of fans—male, female, young, and old—wearing their replica mustaches.

JAGUARS FANS WELCOMED THE TEAM'S NEW OWNER IN STYLE IN DECEMBER 2011

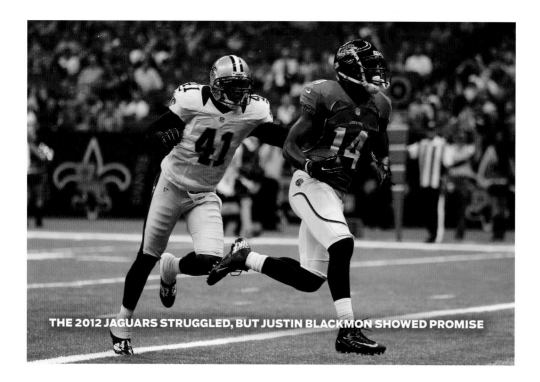
THE 2012 JAGUARS STRUGGLED, BUT JUSTIN BLACKMON SHOWED PROMISE

scored a franchise-low 15.2 points per game on their way to a 5–11 finish.

On the upside, Jones-Drew won the NFL rushing title (1,606 yards), and Jacksonville's defense—led by defensive end Jeremy Mincey, who tallied 8 sacks, 4 forced fumbles, and an interception—showed some bite. When businessman Shahid Khan assumed ownership of the Jaguars in 2012, his main concern was boosting the club's passing attack. To that end, he hired former Atlanta Falcons offensive coordinator Mike Mularkey as Jacksonville's head coach and drafted highly touted wide receiver Justin Blackmon out of Oklahoma State. "This is a team that is very close to making things happen, and I'm here to make sure it does happen," said Mularkey.

Objective observers didn't necessarily share Mularkey's rosy outlook. "There is simply not enough talent here for Mike Mularkey to turn things around right away," said NFL blogger Andy Benoit of *The New York Times* in August 2012. "The offense is at least two years (and probably six or seven players) away, and it's doubtful the defense can overachieve as it did in 2011." Unfortunately for Jaguars fans, Benoit proved to be the better prophet, as Jacksonville won just 2 out of 16 games in 2012 to notch the worst record in franchise history. Apart from Blackmon, the 2012 Draft class provided little help, and the team's management raised eyebrows all around the league when it drafted a punter in the third round despite having so many other areas of need.

Wide receiver Cecil Shorts III had a better year statistically than Blackmon but went largely unheralded in the press. Still, Jacksonville fans recognized that he was the other half of a dynamic pass-catching

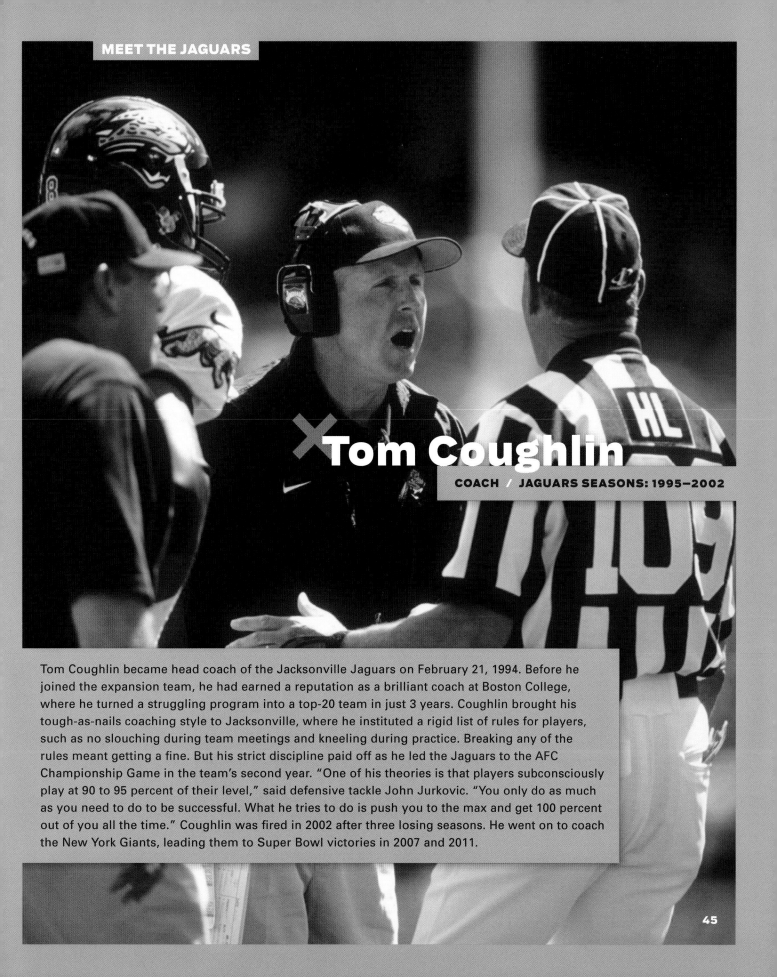

Tom Coughlin

COACH / JAGUARS SEASONS: 1995–2002

Tom Coughlin became head coach of the Jacksonville Jaguars on February 21, 1994. Before he joined the expansion team, he had earned a reputation as a brilliant coach at Boston College, where he turned a struggling program into a top-20 team in just 3 years. Coughlin brought his tough-as-nails coaching style to Jacksonville, where he instituted a rigid list of rules for players, such as no slouching during team meetings and kneeling during practice. Breaking any of the rules meant getting a fine. But his strict discipline paid off as he led the Jaguars to the AFC Championship Game in the team's second year. "One of his theories is that players subconsciously play at 90 to 95 percent of their level," said defensive tackle John Jurkovic. "You only do as much as you need to do to be successful. What he tries to do is push you to the max and get 100 percent out of you all the time." Coughlin was fired in 2002 after three losing seasons. He went on to coach the New York Giants, leading them to Super Bowl victories in 2007 and 2011.

JACKSONVILLE HOPED THAT BLAINE GABBERT WAS THE QUARTERBACK OF THE FUTURE

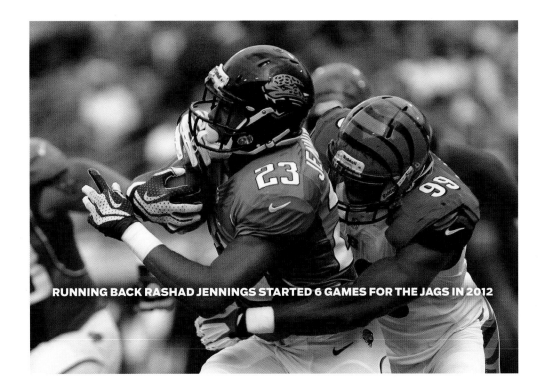

RUNNING BACK RASHAD JENNINGS STARTED 6 GAMES FOR THE JAGS IN 2012

tandem that fans hoped would become a modern version of the Jimmy Smith and Keenan McCardell duo of years past. At season's end, new general manager Dave Caldwell fired Mularkey in favor of Seattle Seahawks defensive coordinator Gus Bradley, whose Seahawks squad had allowed the fewest points of any NFL team in 2012. "Gus more than met every criteria we insisted on from our new head coach, and his intangibles and leadership abilities are exceptional," said Caldwell. "Gus is who the Jaguars need now and in the future."

After the "Touchdown Jaguars!" group spent years on the hunt for an NFL franchise, Jacksonville's cats pounced into the football world, making the playoffs in four of their first five seasons and reaching two AFC Championship Games. But as the dust has settled from that initial onslaught, the Jaguars remain hungry. And while the Jaguars of the past stalked within striking distance of a Super Bowl, a young, new generation is eager for the hunt that will end with an NFL title.

INDEX